Successful Marketing Online The Easy Way!

Marketing Online is Made SIMPLE With
This Step by Step Guide to Success

ISBN-13: 978-1983742682

ISBN-10: 1983742686

Contents

Introduction.. 6

Chapter 1 - Getting Started 7

Overview... 7

Set Goals.. 8

Know Your Product... 8

Chapter 2 - Review the Business 10

Getting the Product to Market 10

Know Your Competition & Your Consumer.............. 11

Chapter 3 - Do Comparative Studies 12

Look at more than One Year................................. 12

Chapter 4 - Research Methods................................ 14

Primary Research... 14

Secondary Research... 15

Chapter 5 - Writing the Business Review.............. 16

What is Good? What is Bad?............................... 16

Is Your Company Working Together? 16

How Will Your Company Market? 17

Where is Your Business Going?.......................... 17

Chapter 6 - Check Your Product and the Market 18

Identify Company Goals...................................... 18

Your Company.. 18

Company Organization.. 19

Sales Data and Trends 19

Chapter 7 - Consumer Trends................................ 21

Consumer Activity... 21

Population Factors 21

Regional Factors 21

Technological Factors 22
Media Factors 22
Chapter 8 - Distribution.. 24
Retail Trends 24
Distribution and Geography 24
Chapter 9 - Marketing and Pricing...................................... 26
Pricing the Product 26
Is Your Product Elastic?... 26
Chapter 10 - Know Your Competition 27
Key Information 27
Marketing Analysis 28
Chapter 11 - Moving Forward.. 29
Sales Objectives 29
Influences on Sales Objectives... 30
Chapter 12 - Defining Your Market 33
Identify Your Target Demographic 33
Separate Your Target Markets... 33
Main Target Market... 34
Secondary Markets 34
Further Segmentation 35
Know the Demand.. 35
Chapter 13 - Positioning Your Product 37
What Positioning Means 37
Is Positioning Important? 37
Chapter 14 - Marketing Strategy 39
Naming Strategy.. 39
Competition Strategy... 39
Product Strategy 40
Packaging Strategy 40
Pricing Strategy 41
Advertising Strategy... 41

Chapter 15 - The Importance of Naming and Packaging . 43

    Naming 43

    Packaging... 44

Chapter 16 - Putting the Plan into Action.......................... 46

    Making the Implementation of Your Plan a Success.... 46

    Stay on Top of the Plan 47

Chapter 17 - Evaluation 48

    General Evaluation 48

    Comparing Sales... 48

    More Research 49

    Follow the Plan 50

Introduction

When you have a business, it is important to be able control the narrative of your product. You will want the product to have a positive image in the minds of consumers. It is up to you and your company to come up with a message that will convey what you feel the product is all about. Doing this is not an easy task. You will have to conduct research, either by yourself or you can hire another company to do it for you. From this research, you will be able to identify a group of consumers that you will target through the marketing campaign and it is this is the group of consumers that the marketing plan will be designed to. Research will also have to be conducted on your industry and any companies that you identify as your competition.

By being diligent with your research and getting the whole company involved you will be able to ensure that the marketing plan that is agreed upon will have the best chance of succeeding because the entire company will feel some ownership of the plan and will work to see its proper implementation. However, perhaps the most important part of coming up with a marketing plan is knowing your product inside and out. You will have to know how it is going to be used by consumers. If there are many uses for the product, if there is only one, or does it work in conjunction with another product or does it stand by itself. Having a clear understanding of the product will help you streamline your marketing campaign and make it that much more effective.

Chapter 1 - Getting Started

One of the key aspects in becoming successful in business is being able to market your company to ensure that you get the most out of it. By being able to successfully get your company's name out to the masses, you will find that you will be able to control what your company stands for more easily and be able to easily maintain a positive brand image.

When you embark on coming up with a marketing plan there are certain areas and steps that you should follow in order to make the marketing campaign a success and making sure that your message is clearly represented and can be easily absorbed by your target audience.

Overview

First, take a good look at your business. You have to make sure that you understand your business clearly, what it is that you want your business to accomplish, more than just bring you profits. By ensuring that you completely understand what it is that you want to do you will be able to form a marketing database. The review of your company needs to be comprehensive to ensure that you get the data necessary to make your marketing campaign successful.

For the best results, make sure that you review your own company records. Bring together your potential customers, have focus groups, and conduct surveys. Make sure you stay up to date with any publications that might be relevant to you company's industry. Get to know the marketplace for your product or service as well as you possibly can. Become informed about your competition and how they go about marketing and who they feel is their target demographic. By doing this you will have the tools you need to make informed decisions about your marketing campaign.

Set Goals

When thinking about your marketing campaign it is imperative that you set sales goals. This is a critical step in your marketing campaign. Without setting a sales goal, you will be at a disadvantage when coming up with the rest of the marketing campaign. By setting a number as a goal it gives you and your team a focus point. If the number is not there, you will not know how much of a product you want manufactured, how to distribute the product in stores, what your budget needs to be, or how much or how little you need to advertise.

Once you have set the sales goal for the product you will need to identify who it is that you want to market your product to. The group of people that you will want to market your product to will most likely fall into the same age bracket, income level, and gender. This will help you to design your marketing campaign to your target demographic and will help you save money by not marketing to a wide audience and wasting your message on consumers who will not be interested in your product.

Know Your Product

After you have identified your target market, the next step is to come up with a marketing plan that will put your product in the best position to be successful. This step is known as brand positioning. When you position the product that you are trying to market, it means that you attempting to control how the public is going to perceive it. In effect, you are telling your target demographic how your product is going to enhance their life and why they should not be without it.

Knowing how your product is going to be positioned in the marketplace you can move forward and determine what kind of strategy you want to pursue when it comes to marketing the product. This is done by incorporating the sales goal numbers that have previously been set. The marketing strategy will put in plain words how these goals are going to be achieved.

When you finally get to implement your marketing campaign you want to stay on top of all the details that went into the plan. This is the most crucial point. If the plan is not executed correctly, all the time and effort that went into it will be for naught. Lastly, when all is said and done you should go back and examine the entire plan and see where things went according to plan and where things might have to be reevaluated or redone.

Chapter 2 - Review the Business

To make things easier when you start to review your business make your self an outline that includes all the areas that you want to study. By making an outline you will be able to make sure that your business review will remain focused on topics that you feel are important to the success of you company. Topics that you should include in the outline are a summery of what your company excels at and what it needs to improve on.

You should then follow with a complete look at what your company stands for, its goals and objectives. This section will also include topics such as the items that are similar to your product that are targeted to the same demographic that you are looking to market to. Make sure that you include a review of sales trends in different areas across the country. Are the sales seasonal? Are there different areas of the country where you product will be more in demand? How does your product stack up against your competitor's product?

Getting the Product to Market

Your outline must include a comprehensive study of how to get your product to consumers. Take a good look at different types of distribution methods, what it will take to get your product to different areas of the country. Packaging should also be reviewed. What type of packaging will make your product more appealing to your target demographic? How much space will your product take up on store selves?

Is your product going to be marketed to consumers or to businesses? These are the type of questions that you need to be able to answer in order to make your outline complete.

When you are thinking about how to get your product to market, one of the most important steps is to figure out what the price of the product is going to be. To make sure that your pricing is competitive you need to review what your competitors are charging for products. You need to know if your product is inelastic or elastic with the economy and all the production and administrative costs that go into making the product.

Know Your Competition & Your Consumer

In addition to pricing and distribution, you need to have an in depth study of your competition included in your outline. You have to know what share of the market they have. How they are marketing their product. Do they advertise on television? On the radio? What about online? Are they known to have good or bad customer service? As well as knowing your company's strengths and weaknesses, it is important to know the same things about all your competitors.

In order to have a successful marketing campaign you must be able to identify and market directly to your target demographic. Having an intricate knowledge of your product should allow you to identify your target demographic by certain factors. These factors should include their age, gender, education level, job, income level, the size of their household, and where they live in the country. You need to know if consumers of this type of product have loyalty to one brand or are they willing to try new brands that appear on the market.

11

Chapter 3 - Do Comparative Studies

To get an accurate idea of the competitive market that you want to enter it is important to have points of reference that you can examine. The best way to do this is to do some comparative studies about your industry as well as your competition. For the best results, it is useful to include five years of information because this will allow your study to be more accurate and give you a better understanding of recent trends in the industry.

Look at more than One Year

By including five years worth of data in your studies, you can avoid pitfalls in your review. This will exclude one-year trends that might show a high spike in sales of a product or that show a product that sales are somewhat stagnant. Five years worth of data will give you a better idea of the trends that are happening in your industry and give you a clear impression of where the industry is going in the years to come.

In addition to your industry, look at a five year trend of your target demographic. You need to know if the same demographic has been buying the product for the last five years or has it been changing. If it has been changing, why has it been changing? Have consumers purchased more than one of the product? If so, was it from the same manufacturer or have they decided on a different company? Was price a factor in the decision to purchase one product from another? It is important for you to know what is influencing your target demographic to purchase a like product so you can design your marketing campaign accordingly.

Be sure to include a study of your competition in the five-year study. By studying your competition you will have a better understanding of the industry. Is the department that makes the product that you will be competing against expanding or contracting? What percentage of the market do they have? Does your competitor market the product locally or across the country? Have their sales gone up, down, or remained consistent over the past five years?

Knowing this information will give you a better idea of how to break into the market. Where the areas of the industry you can exploit are and if there has been any increase in the number of businesses trying to break into the industry. If the industry has become saturated with businesses trying to break into it, it is better to find out now than when you and your company have more time and money invested.

Chapter 4 - Research Methods

When you are preparing your outline and doing a business review there are certain methodologies that you should use when doing your research in order get to most important information and make your study more complete. The main types of research that will be done will be primary and secondary. Each method has its specific use and will contribute to the development of your marketing plan.

Primary Research

One of the most important areas to gather information in primary research is through the use of surveys. When conducting a survey you want to make sure that the sample size is large enough that you will get results that will be statistically accurate. Surveys should be conducted on two levels. The first should focus on your customers, whether they have already purchased from your company or they are the target market that you want to break into. Second, you will want to conduct a market-based survey, which will give you good information about the industry and what consumers are looking for.

Another type of primary research that you should conduct is interviews with potential customers. These can be done in a variety of settings. You can conduct focus groups with varying sizes of consumers to gauge the public's interest in your product. You can have more intimate interviews with a one-on-one setting, or you could try to talk to people on the street or shopping center.

Conducting these types of interviews or group sessions can give good feedback on what the perception of your company is or what the public is looking for in the industry that you are trying to break in to. However, when using this type of data, known as qualitative research, it is best used when you have other data to back up the information from a small group of individuals. This is because a small sampling of people could give you information that would be considered an outlier when combined with better statistical data.

Secondary Research

Secondary research consists of information that is available in published sources. It is up to you to find this information and apply it to your company. To find relevant publications or sources all you will need to do is go to the local public library or if you are close to a college or university you will be able to find these sources in their libraries as well. Another good secondary source for information is the census or the Bureau of Labor and Statistics. These are great sources to use with a wealth of information and it is all available online, free of charge.

Take advantage of these options, not only to save money, but everything that you could think of is broken down is easily obtainable data.

Chapter 5 - Writing the Business Review

Now that you have done all the research or had a company do the research for you it is time to put all the information together in order to make sense of it so you can move forward with your marketing plan.

What is Good? What is Bad?

The first thing that should be included in you business review is a breakdown of what your company is good at and where it needs help. With the information that you have gathered you should be able to identify the advantages that your company has in terms of your target market wants and needs. The advantages your company can take in terms of distributing the product. How efficient your company can be producing the product and how that can be applied to making pricing an advantage. You will also want to identify your products technical advantages over your competition.

Is Your Company Working Together?

From the information that you have gathered you should also be able to determine how well your company works together. If your company is not working together for a common goal you will find the becoming successful is nearly impossible. To be a successful company all departments must be working in concert with each other for a common goal. Management and workers all must have a stake in what to final outcome of the product is. This is best accomplished by a consistent dialogue between both sides.

Having a free flow of ideas between all sides will serve your company well and give you an advantage over your competition, and could even attract the best and brightest in your industry to come and work for you.

How Will Your Company Market?

The information that you have gleaned from several sources should also be able to help you identify how well your company markets itself. The answered surveys can be a key asset here. In the questionnaire there should have been questions asking consumers how they feel about your company and how effectively it gets its message across. Questions should have also included suggestions of how consumers want to be marketed to and what they are looking for in a company.

Where is Your Business Going?

With all the data you have collected the next step is to identify where you want to take your business. You should be able to determine if there are areas or departments inside your business that you feel will benefit from expansion. You should also be able to identify if there other areas that you feel that your business can expand and gain a larger share of the market. The data could also point out that this is not the proper time to focus on expanding. From surveys, you should be able to garner if your target demographic is looking for your company to expand and if they want new products from your company.

Chapter 6 - Check Your Product and the Market

As you continue to prepare your business review there are more areas and steps that you will need to complete in order to make the most informed decisions for your company.

Identify Company Goals

Each company is different and therefore, should have its own unique set of goals that it wants to accomplish. The information that you have gathered through primary and secondary research will help you set the long-term and short-term goals of the company. These goals should include the sales goals of the company, profit goals, and what you expect from marketing campaigns.

The information will also help you understand where to apply the budget across the company. You will be able to set a standard mission statement for the company to focus their efforts and how to go about relating to customers, employees, and developing the product.

Your Company

Put together a summery of your company's history. Include how that company came to be, what it has accomplished to this point. How it has evolved over time. You will want to see if the company has changed its mission. How has expansion or contraction helped or hurt the business. However, it is not only the company history that you want to focus on. You will want to analyze the data you have collected to determine future trends in the industry in order to better position your company.

In order to get an unfettered view of your company the data that you have collected should be able to help you address what plans have been crucial to your company's success, why consumers find your company worth purchasing from, and how your company is viewed by the public.

Company Organization

As well as looking at your company as a whole, you have to be able to look how your company is organized. If you have a marketing department, you must know how well that department works with the rest of your company. Make sure that the marketing department is sufficiently staffed and has the ability to come up with a professional marketing plan and that they have the means to implement the plan. The data that you have collected should also be able to show you how the marketing department has performed in previous campaigns. Responses from interviews will be key into providing information about the message that you have been trying to send about your company and products and if they have been resonating with your target demographic.

Sales Data and Trends

Analyzing sales data will be a large part of the business review. Sales data might be the most important of the analysis that takes place because it will tell you more about consumers than any other information that you have collected. A proper analysis of sales data will show you a definitive picture of sales trends for the industry, your company, your competitor, and who has the greatest market share.

When you are analyzing the sales data, it is important that you have at least five years worth of information to ensure an accurate sampling. By having five years worth of sales data you will be able to identify if sales of like products are increasing, decreasing, or stagnant. The analysis of sales data should also provide information about market share. It will show how much of the market share that you currently have along with if your company's market share has been increasing, decreasing, or stagnant over the last five years.

The analysis of sales data can also be broken down further by analyzing sales data by individual stores. This will help you determine which stores are important to the future of your company and where you might want to think about trying different outlets. When braking down individual store sales your data will be able to show what stores outperformed others and which were below average in terms of sales and profitability.

Sales should also be analyzed by season. This will be able to tell you if the product is more desired at different times of the year. If that is the case, then it will give you a better idea of how and when your product will need help from the marketing department.

Moreover, the five years worth of sales data that you have collected should also be analyzed based on geographic region. This will better ensure that your product is readily available in stores where there is a greater demand for your product, and you will be better able to make sure that the product gets to the regions where you will be better able to make a profit.

Chapter 7 - Consumer Trends

Consumer Activity

Having five years worth of data to analyze is a crucial tool to shed light on the trends of consumers. Once you analyze the data, you will be sure to see that consumers act in certain ways that are affected by region, social, economic, and personal. By being able to analyze these trends with consumers you and your marketing team will have the tools necessary to predict these trends giving your company the ability to better market itself and the product.

Population Factors

When analyzing population factors that affect marketing one of the best tools you can use is the US Census and the Bureau of Labor and Statistics. These web sites have all the information that you need and are free to use online. From these websites you will be able to find the median age of a city, state or region, the education level, and if the population in a given area has increased or decreased in recent years. You will also be able to see what types of households there are in certain areas. When marketing it is important to know if a household is headed by a male or female, are the occupants married, if there are children, if so, how many, along with the income level of the occupants.

Regional Factors

Another great use for the US Census and the Bureau of Labor and Statistics is gleaning information about different areas of the country. By using this data properly, you will be able to see the differences across the country in education levels, income levels, the make up of families, the rate of unemployment, and where different ethnicities are located. All this information will better prepare you to develop a marketing plan that will more easily reach your target demographic and making the marketing campaign a success.

If you analyze the data well it will be able to show you trends in population growth across the country. If your target demographic is moving to certain areas of the country, then it behooves you to market to the areas that they are relocating. This may also affect how you get your product to market so all of this data has to be taken into account when it comes to pricing and business expansion.

Technological Factors

Technology is playing a larger role in everyday life than it ever has before. This is not an area that you can overlook. You should be able to determine if technology is something that you can take advantage of to better help your marketing ability. You will need to know if there have been any advances in technology in your industry and if it can add value to your product. Even advances in technology that are in the area of logistics can greatly help your product if you can more easily keep track of shipments.

Media Factors

Media no longer means the evening news or newspapers. Nowadays, with the explosion of social media consumers can be reached in many ways. Make sure that your marketing team takes a close look how it can boost your company's presence online. Today, almost all companies have a presence on social media sites like Facebook and Twitter. This makes it easier for companies to stay connected to consumers who like their products and it is an inexpensive way for companies to let consumers know about a new product that is coming to market or an upcoming sale on already existing merchandise.

Along with social media, it is important for you to know the percentage of your target demographic that uses traditional types of media. You will need to compare data to see what types of television programs that your target demographic watches and at what times. The same goes for radio stations, newspapers, and magazines. Knowing all this information will help to streamline your marketing campaign to the consumers that you want to influence.

Chapter 8 - Distribution

When putting together your business review, it is important to go over your distribution methods to see if they are the most cost effective and successful. To do this do not only look at your own company but look at how your competitors are getting their products to market.

Retail Trends

The data that you have collected should help you determine what the top methods of distribution are. This will take some dedication on your part when you are analyzing the data for there are many ways of distributing a product. Products can be distributed by department stores, catalogs, direct mail, online, specialty stores, and discount outlets just to name some of the ways. It is up to you to figure out the best way to distribute your product. This is where the five years worth of data can be of help. Having that much data will show you what the current trends of distribution are in your industry.

Distribution and Geography

When determining what distribution methods are the best for your company it is important for you to take geography into account. You research should be able to show you if stores that sell your product are accessible, if they are close to main roads making them easier to get to for consumers. The research should also show if the stores are in areas that do well and turn a profit. You will also be able to see how your competition stacks up to you in the same geographical regions.

Your research will be able to show if you have reached the best possible position for your product. This means have you reached your saturation point with the current levels of outlets that sell your product and should you start looking for other alternatives to get your product to consumers. It will also be able to tell if your current level of market saturation is your optimum level.

The five years worth of research, you will be able to tell where your product is most in demand. What types of stores consumers shop at to purchase your product. If there are any new methods of distribution that are emerging in your industry. Should you start looking to expand to new regions and what type of distribution best fits your company.

Chapter 9 - Marketing and Pricing

Determining a price for your product is an important step when coming up with a marketing plan. If the price is set too low your company will have a hard time making a profit. A price that is set to high could encourage competition, which could hinder the success of your company.

Pricing the Product

To get an idea of how you should price your product there needs to be frequent checks made of your competition and how they are pricing their product. By doing this you will be able to create a history of pricing so you can determine if there are any trends. Having a good history of your competitors pricing will let you know if they change the price at certain times of the year in an effort to boost their sales. This will let you counter their pricing with your own prices keeping you competitive at all times. By looking at your competition, it will help you see supply and demand trends that will help you set a competitive price that will ensure your company the best chance to turn a profit.

Is Your Product Elastic?

Having a good history of pricing will let you know if your product is price elastic. Your product is considered price elastic if the price of the product is raised and the demand for the product decreases. The same is true if the price of the product is lowered and demand for the product goes up. A good source for this information is the surveys that you have completed or from focus groups that you have had done to gauge consumer opinion. Your research should let you know how elastic your product is, and the elasticity of your industry.

Chapter 10 - Know Your Competition

Doing a complete analysis of your completion is a crucial step in determining how to proceed in your marketing campaign. By analyzing your competition, you will have to look at the differences between your company and others. The analysis should also include how your competition markets their product and will give you insight on how you should respond with your marketing campaign. By analyzing your competitions marketing campaigns and strategies you will be able to see where they succeeded and where they failed giving your company an advantage when you implement your marketing campaign.

Key Information

When you are doing a comparative review of your company against your competitors there are certain elements of information that you want to look at. From the information that you have already gathered you will want to compare target markets, sales, pricing, packaging, customer service, marketing objectives, and publicity. The secondary research that you have already done will be the best sources of information when it comes to checking out your competition.

After you have done a complete analysis on your company and your competition you will be able to know the market share of your competitors in relation to your company. How your competitors distribute their product. Their marketing strategies, and where they were successful and where they were not. You will be able to determine if they have a loyal customer base or whether consumers of their products have looked elsewhere.

Marketing Analysis

Your comparative analysis should include an in depth look at your company and competitors marketing campaigns. After you have completed the review of your company and your competitors you will be able to get a clear understanding of your products strengths and weaknesses in comparison to the competition. You will also be able to see any trends in market share and sales. What percentage of the target demographic account for sales and is this the same target demographic as your competition. You will get a better understanding of your company's marketing strategies and how they are like or different from your competitors.

In addition, you will be able to compare your products pricing to that of your competitors. You will also be able to know how your customer service stacks up against your rivals. You will see if your company relies on marketing more or less than the competition and you will see if your marketing campaigns were successful to driving business away from your competitors to your company.

Chapter 11 - Moving Forward

Now that you have completed the business review its time to prepare the marketing plan. The first step in this process is to set sales objectives. This is not as easy as its sounds, no random number will do, and it will take time and effort to project a proper sales objective.

Sales Objectives

The entire marketing plan will be designed on meeting the sales objectives, which is why this step is first and crucial to get right. Because sales are so important to a company the objectives must be simultaneously demanding and achievable. The sales objectives must be set by giving a precise estimate of the opportunities that exist in the marketplace along with the ability of the company to meet those estimates. By setting sales objectives too high you will also be putting more pressure on the entire organization and increasing the cost of running the company. If sales objectives are too low, the company will have a hard time keeping products in stock and meeting consumer demand. Sales objectives that are not accurate will put a strain on your company that is avoidable.

As well as being demanding and achievable sales objectives must be time specific. This will give your marketing team a start date and an end date. Short-term sales objectives are usually designed for up to twelve months and long-term goals are designed for up to three years.

Remember what is included in the short-term marketing plan will affect sales for the years after the first. Therefore, if your company is designing new products to be released they should be tested in the first year so by the third year they will be able to reach sales objectives.

The sales objectives that have been set must be able to be measured. How you plan on measuring the sales objectives should be included in the marketing plan. There are several ways that you can make the objectives measurable. It can be done in terms of money, units, and transactions. Measuring with money indicates the expenses that you have incurred making the product; the profits made, and will also show any elasticity of the product if there were any price fluctuations. When you measure with units and transactions, it will show how well your product is being received by consumers. Sales objectives must also include a projection of profits because sales have a direct influence on profits.

Influences on Sales Objectives

Your research will come in handy when setting sales objectives. A review of the marketplace over the past five years will show any upward, downward, variable, or static trends. Analyze how sales at your company are moving on a yearly basis in comparison to sales in the entire marketplace. This will give you an idea of how to project sales in the future. Sales should be projected at least equal and perhaps a little ahead of market growth in order for your company to maintain its share.

You will also need to review your data for any trends that you can see in your company's share of the market. If you find that your company's share of the market has been changing, whether it has been increasing or decreasing you will be able to adjust your sales projections accordingly.

If you find that the market is in decline or your market share is in decline be aware that this is something that is extremely difficult to turn around.

Additionally, to be able to set proper sales objectives it is good to review your company's history in terms of annual budgets and expected profits. This will at least give a minimum number to start with because sales of your product will need to cover operating expenses. If prices change during the year, at holiday's for example, these need to be factored into your sales objectives.

One factor that is difficult for any business to predict when it comes to sales objectives is the economy. The best you can do is analyze the data that you have a set the sales objectives to an estimation of what you feel the economy is going to do. Along with trying to predict the economy, you must also keep a close watch on interest rates. Interest rates are important to companies because customers use credit many times to purchase goods. If interest rates go up consumers are going to tighten their purse strings and not buy goods.

Moreover, another factor that can influence sales objectives is your competition. If you are part of a growing market it might attract more competition so be sure to know who you are up against before finalizing your sales objectives. In addition, instead of more business competing against you it could be an old competitor that is looking to increase their market share and trying to push you out, so you will have to respond to their challenge.

The last factor that you want to address when setting your sales objective is the product itself. Every product on the market has a life of its own and it is up to you to determine where your product is in theirs. If your product has been on the market for several years you will want to take that into account because your market might be smaller because people already have the product. Conversely, you might be introducing a new or improved product that has a vast untapped market.

Chapter 12 - Defining Your Market

To ensure that you reach the sales objectives that you have set it is important to know who your target market is and what their purchasing history has been.

Identify Your Target Demographic

When you were gathering information and doing your business review possible target markets were identified. The target demographic is a portion of consumers that have like buying habits, economic factors, education level, and need for the product. By identifying your target market you will able to better streamline your marketing campaign to them to increase their chances of buying your product. It is important not to try to market to every single consumer otherwise you will missing out on the segment of society that is interested in what you are selling.

Separate Your Target Markets

After you have identified different target markets you will want to put them in different categories so you will be able to manage them better. This will help you better target the common characteristics of similar groups. You will be better able to market to the groups as though they were individuals. One of the most common ways businesses separate target markets is to put them a current customer category and a potential customer category. This will help you think of marketing campaigns that will keep current customers interested in your company and make them repeat consumers and how you can attract the segment of society that you have deemed potential customers to try your product.

Main Target Market

Your main target market is the group of consumers that is currently using your product. These consumers are your bread and butter because they are already familiar with your company and products so it is important to keep them coming back. It is important for your main target market group to be large enough to sustain your company. Your main target market should be responsible for thirty to sixty percent of total sales of your product. It is important to keep up to date with your main target market so you will be able to quickly identify any trends in their buying habits.

Secondary Markets

While your marketing plan will mainly focus on the main target group, it is important to identify secondary target market groups because they can add extra sales and add to your company's profitability. Secondary markets can be made up of different types of consumers. It could be a group of consumers that could fit into your main target group but there are not enough of them in a certain area at present but have the potential to grow into a larger segment. Perhaps your target market is for males aged thirty-five to fifty-five but twenty somethings like the product as well, the twenty somethings would be a secondary market because there would not ne enough of them to sustain your businesses profitability.

Further Segmentation

Target markets are further divided into other groups. One of the most popular groups that businesses put consumers is by their buying habits. Consumers are put into this category based on if a product is purchased more than one time per year, what time of year is the product purchased, and how the product is used.

Consumers are also put into categories based on their lifestyle. Factors that are identified are a consumer's interests, habits, education, income level, and employment. If you can identify a fair sized group that enjoys fishing, for example, you will better be able to reach them by advertising in outdoor themed magazines, hunting programs, or at bait and tackle shops.

Where a person lives also plays a part into consumers buying habits. It is important to remember that in different areas of the country consumers have different interests based on the topography, weather, income, and opportunity. This comes in handy if you are selling a product that relies on weather to be useful, whether it is sunny or snowy. You will have to adjust your marketing campaign accordingly to reach your company's sale objectives.

Know the Demand

The last thing that you will need to do after identifying your target market is to analyze the demand for your product. This will let you know if the group that you have selected to be your main market group is large enough to sustain your company. When analyzing the demand for your product there are several factors that you will want to identify. You will want to know the average amount of time a consumer purchases your product on an annual basis. Will there be any restrictions on your product that will make it unavailable to some consumers. You will also need to know what your company's market share is and how much of your product is purchased in different geographic regions.

Chapter 13 - Positioning Your Product

Now that you have completed your sales objectives and identified your main and secondary target markets it is time to put your product in the best possible position to succeed and fit in to the overall marketing strategy.

What Positioning Means

When you are trying to position your product, you are attempting to put the image of your product in the minds of consumers who you have targeted to purchase your product. If done correctly it will put your characterization of the product in the minds of the target market ahead of your competition. Putting your product in a good position will help consumers view your product differently than your competition.

Is Positioning Important?

When coming up with a marketing plan, positioning the product is important. Having good product positioning is the base for all of your activity with consumers. Without having good product positioning your communication, advertising, merchandising, and publicity will all suffer. When you are marketing your product, you are reinforcing your product positioning. All these areas of your business must work together to convey the common message of the position of your product.

When you are looking towards the long-term positioning of your product there are some factors that you must address. You must understand what your target group wants from your product and you should have a clear understanding of your competition. The research that you have already done will be a great help to you when it come to positioning your product. Having a good understanding of your products strengths and weaknesses in relation to your competition is good place to start when positioning your product. Having a good idea of what separates your product from your competition will help you position your product as well.

Along with the research that you have done on the strengths and weaknesses of your product that will help position your product, the research that you have done on your target market will be of equal help. The surveys and interviews that you conducted will be of use here because they were conducted directly with consumers. This is because no matter what you do, the target market must be put first, and any positioning must be focused on them.

Furthermore, in order to position your product in the best way by using your target market these are the questions you should have the answers to through your research. Why the target market is buying, is it that your product is the best or is your brand name associated with quality products? Where is most of the product purchased? Does in vary by geographic region or season? Is your product meant to be used with another product or is it a stand alone product? Is it a product that will be purchased frequently or infrequently? Knowing this information about your target market will go along way into putting your product in the best position to succeed.

Chapter 14 - Marketing Strategy

A marketing strategy is a plan that will show how your marketing objectives are going to be fulfilled. When coming up with a marketing strategy you will want to consider the following factors: naming, competition, the product, markets, packaging, pricing, and advertising.

Naming Strategy

If your company is planning on releasing a new product, you will need to give a route for the name of the new product. This means that if it is a new product do you want to try and include the name of the product as an offshoot of another product from your company that is already on the market or do you want the name of the product to be something that makes it a stand alone product? Additionally, you will have to decide if the name is something that will keep current customers using your company's products or if you want to give the product a name that will attract a new target market.

Competition Strategy

Competitive strategies can focus on one main competitor or your closest group of competitors. When using a competitive strategy it is best to find something that your company does well and focus on the aspect of your business to set yourself apart from your competition. You may also find that you will be forced to use a competitive strategy when one of your competitors tries to move into a market that your company has been dominant. Think of this as a boxer that is a counter puncher, so when your competition tries to hit you first, your company knows what is coming and reacts hard and fast knocking out the competition before they know what's hit them. Competitive strategies can also be used when introducing a new product where you can incorporate packaging, product improvements, and merchandising to help you gain advantage over your competition.

Product Strategy

Another marketing strategy that you will have to consider is product strategy. When your company is introducing a new product or a product that goes with an already established product line, you will have to make a decision on how to ensure that the product makes an impact when it gets to market.

If you start to notice things like your product is not selling as well as it used to and consumer confidence appears to be slipping about your company you have to make the decision on how to turn public opinion around so you can reach your sales objectives. If you have a product that might have limited use, you can look to try to find alternate uses for your product and introduce them to your target market.

Packaging Strategy

You might think that if you have a good product that does what you say it will do and does it well is all that you would need to make your product a success. However, that is not the case. Many products will be chosen from store shelves just because of their packaging. When it comes to packaging your product there are certain factors that you need to address. The packaging is first and foremost a way to protect the product. Second, packaging should add some value to the product. If a consumer sees the care that the company has taken in packaging the product they will understand that the company feels that they have a quality product and they will feel the same way. Packaging is also a great way for your company to get its message across and perhaps entice other markets than your main target market to try the product.

Pricing Strategy

When you are looking at marketing strategies, you should look at pricing as an option. You will have to decide whether you want to attack your competition by either pricing your product higher or lower than them. You will have to keep in mind that pricing has a direct affect on the sustainability of the business and you will want to make sure that your pricing does not interfere will the chance of turning a profit. Geography also has to be taken into account when using a pricing strategy. The decision has to be made if the product is going to have the same price across each market or will prices vary. Finally, your previously done research should be able to tell you if price is an important factor for your target group to purchase your product.

Advertising Strategy

When you are coming up with a marketing strategy and are looking at what to do with advertising the important thing to remember is that the advertising message should have a consistent message. The main reason for having a consistent message is to show direction for all marketing plans that will derive from your strategies. Therefore, when you make the decision to advertise make sure that in whatever types of media you choose the message is consistent and addresses your target market.

Chapter 15 - The Importance of Naming and Packaging

Perhaps the most important part of your product being in the best position to succeed is naming and packaging. The name of the product along with the packaging is most likely what your target market is going to come into contact first so they must be enticing to them.

Naming

When you name you product, you are giving it an identifying mark that separates it from its competition. The name of the product is there for the consumer to be able to separate like products from each other and they will hopefully associate the name of your product with quality. If this is the case, when they return to the store the will look specifically for your product avoiding your competition.

When you are developing the name for the product, you need to take into account what the product does, the age range of the target market. The name should be kept as simple as possible so that it is easy for consumers to remember. Stay away from names that could be perceived as negative, the name should evoke something positive in the mind of consumers when they hear it or read it.

It is a good idea when it comes to naming your product to have some variations of what you think good names are for the product when you conduct the initial focus groups. This way you will have direct feedback from potential consumers and you will know if you are on the right direction or not. Another interesting way of generating names for your product is to include your employees, this is a great way of getting the whole organization involved and taking ownership of the product and you could give a prize or bonus to the employee who comes up with the name that is chosen.

Packaging

Packaging your product goes hand in hand with your marketing strategy. When the package is being designed the colors of the package, the graphics, and the material used to create the package all has to be in concert with how you want to position your product.

You should think of the package as part of the product. Without having an interesting looking package your product might be entirely overlooked by consumers. As stated previously, the package is many time the first contact that you will have will consumers so it needs to be able to grab their attention. Most importantly, the packaging must appeal to your target market. So take into account the age range of your target market because the same type of graphics and packaging will not appeal to all age ranges.

Perhaps one of the most important parts of packaging is that has a direct impact on consumers attitudes towards your product. If you packaging is memorable, consumers will know your product without even seeing the name. That does not mean that the packaging should be something bizarre and outlandish but it should be something that is functional and adds value to your product. For example, consumers know a Nike brand of shoes just by the color of the shoebox and the swoosh logo; they do not have to see the word Nike to know what it is. They know that they are going to get a quality shoe just by the packaging.

Chapter 16 - Putting the Plan into Action

Now that you have completed the marketing plan, it is time to put your plan into action. This is a time when everyone involved has to be working together to ensure the proper implementation of the plan because if you drop the ball now all of your company's hard work will be for naught.

Making the Implementation of Your Plan a Success

First, your company has to make sure that there are enough assets allocated to ensure a through implementation of the marketing plan. Having representatives from all departments involved in the implementation of the marketing plan will help you if something is not going to plan because a member of that department will be available to correct it on the fly. In addition, having employees from all departments that were involved in forming the marketing plan will help them take ownership of the plan and they will give their best effort in doing a good job.

Second, make sure that all departments that are going to participate in the implementation of the marketing plan have enough time to prepare their contribution. On average, it is a good idea to give departments anywhere from two to four months to ensure that they are ready for the marketing push and that they have time to finish other business so it does not interfere with the implementation of the plan.

Finally, it is your job as head of the company to know what all of the departments are responsible for and how they fit into the overall plan. This is of the upmost importance because if you do not know if something is not going to plan you will not know until its too late and by then it might be unable to be corrected resulting in the failure of the product to be successful.

Stay on Top of the Plan

Implementation of a marketing plan is an ongoing operation. It is not something that works without the vigilance of all involved. This being the case it will help your marketing plan be successful if you develop a timeline of when certain elements of the plan need to be completed. Make sure that the representative department has agreed upon the dates that you set so that the date cannot be easily changed. By having set dates, it will help keep the marketing plan fresh in employees' minds and will show that they are on the road to completing the task.

Chapter 17 - Evaluation

Once the marketing plan has been implemented, it is time see how the plan worked. A good evaluation of the marketing plan will help to provide insight on how to proceed with upcoming marketing plans.

General Evaluation

When you do the evaluation of your marketing plan there are certain areas that you will want to look at to see how successful they were in getting your message across to the consumer. When you do a general evaluation of your marketing plan, you will want to look to see if you reached the sales objectives, how well the message was communicated, and if you reached the profit goal.

The easiest data to evaluate will be if you reached sales objectives and profit goals. This is because you will see the information coming directly back to your company from stores and orders for your product. You will probably have good information on how well you did with your target market as well. Having good information of your target market will help you have an idea of how well your message resonated with them.

Comparing Sales

One way to see how well your marketing campaign worked is to compare sales from the previous year to when your marketing plan was implemented. The evaluation should include comparisons from sales from the time prior, during, and after the marketing plan. This will be able to tell you if sales increased, decreased, or remained stagnant. This should show you any trends that happened during your marketing plan and how effective your message was received by your target market. By evaluating sales trends after the marketing plan was implemented, it will show you if your marketing plan has any long-term effect on the sale of your product.

More Research

Once the marketing plan has been completed it is back to doing more research. When you were putting together the business review, you should have conducted surveys and focus groups to gauge the interest of consumers in your new or improved product. You should do the same thing after the marketing plan has finished. This will give you direct contact and feedback from consumers of your product. You should include people that both bought your product and those consumers who did not in order to understand why they were not interested. Was it because they were not in your target market or was it another reason why your marketing efforts did not sway them to try your product.

Doing the primary research again will so you how good the information that you received in the initial surveys and focus groups was helpful in coming up with your target market and the development of the overall marketing plan. Another part of doing surveys and focus groups before and after the marketing campaign will also show you if consumer attitude and awareness of your product has gotten better, worse, or stayed the same.

Follow the Plan

By following the steps that are outlined here, you will be able to make an effective marketing plan. An effective marketing plan can be a major influence on your business and can help you expand your market share if implemented correctly. You will your sales and profits will have to opportunity to grow, consumers will see your company that is one that has quality products and will feel more positive when purchasing your product.